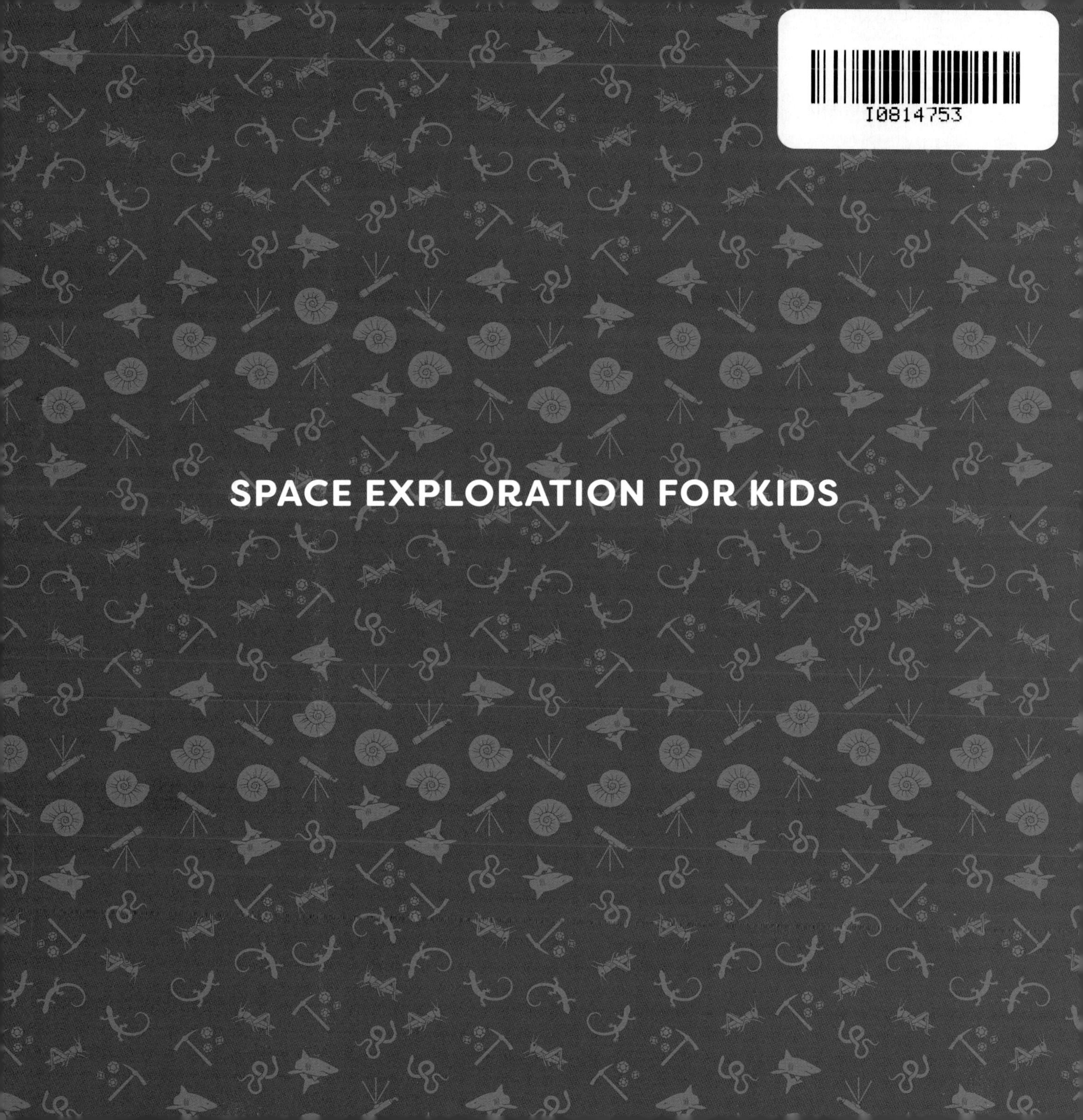
SPACE EXPLORATION FOR KIDS
I0814753

Earth seen from space while astronauts work outside the International Space Station.

SPACE EXPLORATION FOR KIDS

A JUNIOR SCIENTIST'S GUIDE
to Astronauts, Rockets, and Life in Zero Gravity

BRUCE BETTS, PH.D.

ROCKRIDGE PRESS

For my sons, Daniel and Kevin

For general information on our other products and services or to obtain technical support, please contact our Customer Care Department within the United States at (866) 744-2665, or outside the United States at (510) 253-0500.

Rockridge Press publishes its books in a variety of electronic and print formats. Some content that appears in print may not be available in electronic books, and vice versa.

Interior and Cover Designer: Jennifer Hsu
Art Producer: Tom Hood
Editor: Aarti Kelapure
Production Editor: Matt Burnett

Illustrations © Conor Buckley, 2020; Photographs: Vladi333/Nasa/Shutterstock, cover; NASA, pp ii, viii, ix, x, 1, 5, 6, 7, 8, 10, 13, 23, 24, 28, 31, 32, 34, 40, 41, 44, 45, 46, 47, 48, 56, 57, 58, 59, 60, 61, 67, 68; Christina Koch/NASA, p. vi; Archive Image/Alamy, p. viii; SPUTNIK/Alamy, p. viii; J Marshall - Tribaleye Images/Alamy, pp ix, 33; NASA/Roscosmos, p. 2; NASA/Alamy, pp 12, 17, 18, 19, 34, 49, 50, 52, 55; NASA/Bill Ingalls, pp 14, 15; Lauren Harnett/NASA/JSC, p. 16; NASA/Dembinsky Photo Associates/Alamy, pp 20, 37; NASA/Kim Shiflett, p. 20; NASA/Joel Kowsky, pp 26, 27, 29; mccool/Alamy, p. 54; Niday Picture Library/Alamy, p. 55; World History Archive/Alamy, p. 56; NASA Image Collection/Alamy, pp ii, 57, 58; PR Images/Alamy, p 59; Victor Zelentsov, pp 64, 65.

ISBN: Print 978-1-64739-756-2 | eBook 978-1-64739-457-8

R1

Printed in China

CONTENTS

NASA astronaut Andrew Morgan conducts a spacewalk outside the International Space Station.

WELCOME, JUNIOR SCIENTIST!

Do you dream of being an **astronaut**? Do you wonder what astronauts do while in space? Maybe you are curious about what space smells like. If you have questions like these, this book was written with you in mind! Join me as we explore what life is like when you are an astronaut.

Who am I? I'm a guy who loves space so much that I became a planetary scientist. Planetary scientists study the planets, their moons, and even asteroids and comets. I realized I really love teaching and getting people excited about space. That's why I wrote this book.

Humans go to space for many reasons. For one thing, we are curious and love to learn things we don't know much about. What we learn from exploring space helps all people—sometimes in surprising ways. Space exploration helps us develop new technologies and make scientific discoveries. By working together with people all over the world, astronauts inspire people on Earth. Maybe you are one of those people!

In this book, we'll learn what space is and what it means to be an astronaut. You'll see how astronauts train and what they pack for space trips. You will find out what it's like to blast off into space and what it's like to live in a **space station**. Who has gone to space? You will find out that humans aren't the only creatures to make the trip. Finally, you will learn about what you can do now to help prepare you to be an astronaut someday!

Did you know you are already a space traveler? You are on Earth zipping through space as it revolves, or travels, around the Sun. Are you ready to travel beyond Earth? Let's go!

A Brief History of Space Exploration

APRIL 12, 1961:

Yuri Gagarin becomes the first human in space.

MAY 5, 1961:

Alan Shepard Jr. becomes the first American in space.

JUNE 16, 1963:

Valentina Tereshkova becomes the first woman in space.

MARCH 18, 1965:

Alexei Leonov takes the first spacewalk.

MARCH 16, 1966:

First docking, or connection, of two spacecraft in space as part of the Gemini 8 mission.

DECEMBER 24, 1968:

Astronauts first fly around the Moon during the Apollo 8 mission.

JULY 20, 1969:

Neil Armstrong becomes the first human to walk on the Moon during the Apollo 11 mission. Buzz Aldrin becomes the second to do so on that mission.

APRIL 19, 1971:

The first space station, Salyut 1, is **launched**.

DECEMBER 14, 1972:

Humans walk on the Moon for the last time during the Apollo 17 mission.

MAY 14, 1973:

Skylab, the first American space station, is launched.

JULY 17, 1975:

First time two spacecraft from different countries dock together. This was part of the Apollo-Soyuz mission.

APRIL 12, 1981:

First Space Shuttle flight.

JUNE 18, 1983:

Sally Ride becomes the first American woman in space.

FEBRUARY 20, 1986:

First piece of the Mir space station is launched.

NOVEMBER 20, 1998:

First parts of the International Space Station (ISS) are launched.

NOVEMBER 2, 2000:

First time astronauts stay on board the ISS. Many astronauts have stayed there continuously since then.

SEPTEMBER 29, 2011:

First Chinese space station, Tiangong-1, is launched.

MAY 30, 2020:

Launch of the first Crew Dragon spacecraft on a Falcon 9 spacecraft to the ISS. This was the first crewed orbital launch operated by a commercial provider (SpaceX) and the first from the US since the shuttle retirement in 2011.

Madagascar as seen from space.

Chapter One

WHAT TO EXPECT IN SPACE

Where is space? Space is everything beyond the Earth's **atmosphere**. To go to space, astronauts travel in **spacecraft**. This kind of journey takes special equipment and lots of planning. For example, space does not have air to breathe, so astronauts must take air with them. In this chapter, we'll learn what it is like to fly in space. We'll start by exploring what exactly space is. Then, we'll talk about what space feels like, looks like, sounds like, and even smells like. Let's jump in!

Distance in Space

Space is huge! It's so big that a spacecraft would take many years to reach the farthest **planets** in our own **solar system**. A spacecraft traveling to the nearest star outside our solar system would take thousands of years to get there. Astronauts have not traveled that far yet. They fly in space but stay much closer to Earth.

Where exactly does space begin? Most scientists agree that space starts 62 miles above Earth's surface. You can't drive a car to space, but imagine you could. If you drove straight up at freeway speed, it would take about an hour to reach space.

When you reach the edge of space, there is almost no air. Air is what we breathe on Earth. All the air around the Earth is called the atmosphere. The higher we go in the atmosphere, the less air there is. This is why it can be harder to breathe in the mountains.

The International Space Station (ISS).

When we travel high enough to reach the point where there is almost no air, we have reached space. Astronauts need **rockets** to take them that high. They need to wear special **spacesuits** to let them breathe. We'll learn about those later.

The International Space Station (ISS), where a few astronauts are living right now, is about 250 miles up. A space station is a home in space for astronauts. The ISS **orbits** the Earth. That means it goes around and around the Earth without coming down.

When a rocket takes humans or supplies to the ISS, it has to go up hundreds of miles. But it also has to go fast enough to orbit the Earth. To do this, the rocket has to go about 17,500 miles per hour. That's *really* fast! It is so fast that the rocket—and astronauts onboard—travel all the way around the Earth in just an hour and a half. That is about how long it takes you to watch a movie.

The Moon is much farther away than the International Space Station—about 1,000 times farther! It is about

A DEEPER LOOK

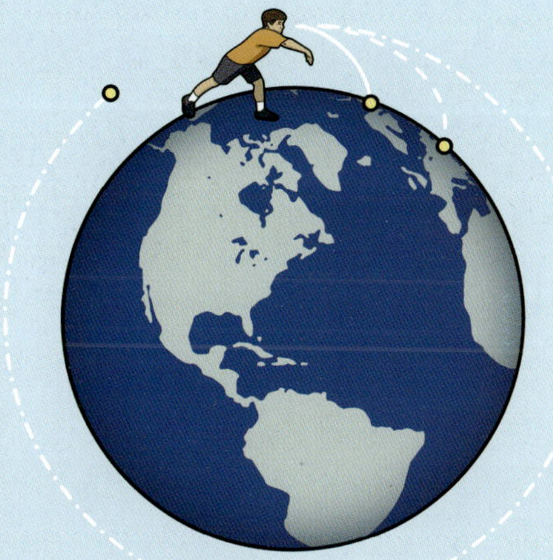

Why doesn't the ISS fall out of space? To understand this, it is helpful to know a little bit about **gravity**. Gravity is the force that keeps you on the ground. When you drop something, gravity is what causes it to fall. If you throw a ball, it still falls, but it travels forward before it hits the ground. The faster you throw the ball, the farther it goes before hitting the ground. If you could throw it superfast, the ball would keep traveling and falling but never hit the ground. A spacecraft has to go very, very fast to stay in orbit. Then it can "fall" around the Earth without coming down. Try the activity later in the chapter (page 9) to learn more.

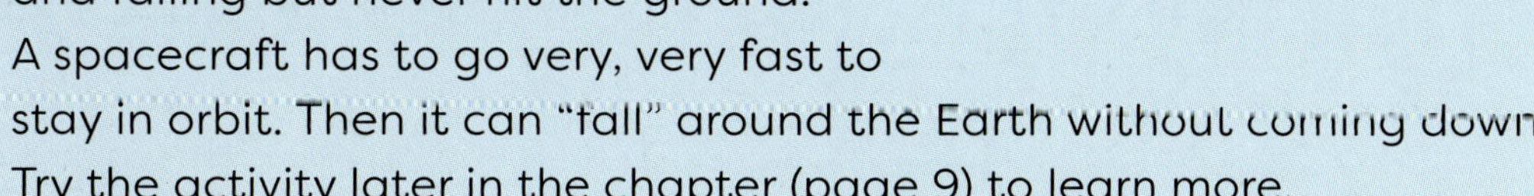

250,000 miles from Earth. This means it is a lot harder to travel there. When astronauts went to the Moon, it took them more than three days to get there.

Mars is more than 150 times farther from Earth than the Moon is. Someday, we may send astronauts to Mars. It will take them seven months or longer to get there. That's a long time on a spacecraft!

DID YOU KNOW?

A rocket takes about eight or nine minutes to propel a spacecraft into space.

THE SCALE OF SPACE

The moon is approximately 250,000 miles from Earth.

The center of the Earth is approximately 3,958 miles down below the surface.

Our Senses in Space

Once you are in space, what is it like? To answer that, let's learn about how astronauts experience space with their five senses.

What does space look like? In most directions, space is black. It looks like the sky you see when you look up on a clear night. During the day on Earth, sunlight bounces around the atmosphere and makes the sky look blue. There is no atmosphere in space, so there is nothing for light to bounce off of. Everywhere astronauts look is black except when they look toward the Sun (which is still extremely bright), the Earth, or the Moon.

Astronauts have a beautiful view of the Earth from space. They can see bright blue oceans, puffy white clouds, and the many different colors of land. They can even see lightning and cities sparkling at night.

Sunrise as seen from the International Space Station. The structure is part of one of the solar arrays that provide power to the ISS.

On Earth, we have one sunrise and one sunset per day. This is because Earth rotates, or spins around, once every 24 hours. Astronauts on the ISS circle the Earth every 90 minutes. This means they see a sunrise every 90 minutes as they move from the night side to the day side of the Earth.

Forty-five minutes later, they see a sunset. How cool is that?

How does space feel? Have you ever let yourself float in water? That's kind of what it feels like in space. Astronauts float inside their spacecraft—and so does everything else. Tools float. Food floats. Even water floats! Nothing falls to the floor.

Space itself is extremely cold—less than -450 degrees Fahrenheit. When a spacecraft is blocked from the Sun, it gets very cold. As the spacecraft moves into the Sun's light, it heats up quickly. Astronauts don't actually feel

Astronaut Jessica Meir floats inside the ISS. Note the floating wrench.

A DEEPER LOOK

The Earth's gravity is almost as strong on the ISS as it is on the ground. Things on the ISS act like there is no gravity, which is sometimes referred to as "zero gravity," because everything is falling all the time. Since there is no air rushing past the astronauts and no changes in speed, they don't feel like they are falling. The only thing they feel is weightlessness—the feeling of floating.

the temperatures of space. They live in a spacecraft that controls the temperature so it is never too hot or too cold. When an astronaut goes outside the spacecraft in a spacesuit, the spacesuit controls the temperature.

What does space sound like? Space itself is silent. Why? Sound needs something to travel through—something like air or water. Space has almost nothing in it—not even air—so sound can't travel. Lots of space movies have scenes with loud sounds outside of the spacecraft, but if you were really in space, you would not hear anything.

Astronauts can hear sound because there is air in their spacecraft and in their spacesuits. They can hear fans or other machines. They can also hear the spacecraft's rockets firing when they are inside. But most of the time, the rockets are off and a spacecraft or space station just moves along silently.

What does space smell like? This seems like a weird question. But astronauts often say that they can smell something on their suits when they take them off. Some say space smells like cooked steak, or toasted almonds.

What does space taste like? Well, an astronaut can't really take a bite of space, but they do eat food just like you do. Sometimes things don't have as much flavor in space, so some astronauts prefer spicy foods while on a space mission.

Food tastes like food but floats in space. Astronaut Julie Payette floats along with a tortilla, a jar, and a knife on board a space shuttle.

A Hubble Space Telescope image of distant, colorful nebulae: huge clouds of gas and dust.

JUNIOR SCIENTISTS IN ACTION

Make your own orbiting spacecraft to learn about orbits!

MATERIALS:

- **STRONG TAPE**
- **3 FEET OF STRING OR THIN RIBBON**
- **1 SMALL BALL, LIKE A TENNIS BALL (OR A SMALL STUFFED ANIMAL)**

ACTIVITY:

Have an adult help you tie or tape one end of the string securely to the ball. The ball is your spacecraft. The string represents Earth's gravity.

Go outside or somewhere with a lot of room and nothing breakable nearby.

Hold one end of the string and begin to spin the ball either in front of you or over your head.

Notice when you spin the ball fast enough, the string straightens out. The string is holding the ball in orbit just as gravity holds the ISS in orbit.

A large telescope.
The Palomar 200 inch.

REACHING FOR THE STARS

Until 400 years ago, people could only explore space from the ground using their eyes. Dutch eyeglass-maker Hans Lippershey changed that in 1608 when he designed the first **telescope**. Telescopes use curved lenses or mirrors to make faraway things appear bigger. Italian **astronomer** Galileo Galilei was the first to study the sky with a telescope. He saw mountains and craters on the Moon and discovered the large moons of Jupiter.

Since Galileo, telescopes have gotten much bigger and much better. Astronomers use them to study many things in space, including planets, stars, and galaxies. Today, there are many huge telescopes working on Earth. There are even some telescopes in space! The Hubble Space Telescope orbits the Earth to study the universe. It doesn't have to look through the fuzzy atmosphere, so it can "see" better than telescopes on the ground.

Even with great telescopes, scientists dreamed of even better views. Sixty years ago, they began sending **robotic spacecraft** out into space. These spacecraft have explored our solar system from Mercury to Pluto and beyond. They have landed on the Moon, on Mars, on asteroids, and on Saturn's moon Titan.

The more scientists discovered with telescopes, the more they wanted to explore and study space in person. So, humans built rockets and spacecraft and learned how to send humans into space. That is how astronauts came to be! The word astronaut means "sailor of the stars."

The Hubble Space Telescope seen floating in Earth orbit. The picture was taken from the space shuttle Discovery.

A robot spacecraft picture of Pluto.

NASA astronaut Scott Kelly inside a Soyuz simulator.

Chapter Two

COUNTDOWN TO LAUNCH!

How do astronauts prepare for a mission to space? You are about to find out! Astronauts must learn many skills before they board their rocket. They need to learn how to use the special equipment in their spacecraft and how to put on their spacesuits properly. It can be difficult to do even simple things without the effects of gravity, so astronauts practice what they will do in space while they're still here on Earth. Let's learn about how astronauts get ready to go to space and what they pack to bring with them.

Astronaut Training

How does someone become an astronaut in the first place? Some astronauts begin as scientists or engineers first. Others start as pilots or doctors. No matter what they learn first, once a person is chosen to be an astronaut, they have to learn a lot more. They have to learn how to live and work in space. They have to learn how to be astronauts!

Someone who wants to be an astronaut spends most of their first two years of training in classrooms learning from teachers. They are taught about life in space, rockets, spacecraft, and space stations. They also learn about the Earth and about other sciences that could help them as astronauts.

Some astronauts may need to learn another language. Those who stay on board the International Space Station should know English and Russian so they can talk with mission control centers in the United States and Russia.

Astronauts during wilderness survival training.

DID YOU KNOW?
Russian astronauts are called **cosmonauts**.

Not all of the early training astronauts do is in the classroom. They need to learn how to fly jet airplanes and

Astronaut Peggy Whitson floats underwater in a spacesuit for ISS EVA spacewalk maintenance training.

practice scuba diving underwater. New astronauts are even sent to the wilderness with only a few supplies and some fellow astronauts as part of their training. They must learn how to survive in the wild on Earth. If their spacecraft lands somewhere unexpected when they return from space, they will know how to take care of themselves.

Astronauts-in-training learn how to use the machines in spacecraft and the ISS before they get into the real thing. They practice in a full-size model of the ISS. This way, astronauts can get used to the ISS before they ever go to space. They learn where things are and how things work by practicing in the model.

To learn how the weightlessness of space feels, astronauts ride in an airplane that flies up, then down quickly. While the plane is flying downward fast, the astronauts feel 20 to 30 seconds of weightlessness as they "fall."

Astronauts also use a huge swimming pool to go on pretend spacewalks. Their spacesuits keep them from floating or sinking in the water. To the person inside the suit, this feels a lot like floating in space.

Astronauts also use virtual reality (VR) in their training. VR is a little like a video game that uses special goggles. VR gives the astronaut a lifelike, 3D view of a pretend world. This lets astronauts practice dangerous things they will do in space in a safe way.

After their first two years of training, astronauts are *still* not ready to go to space. They are usually assigned jobs to do. They may be asked to talk to the astronauts on a space mission or they may work with a company that is building something new to use in space. Whatever the astronauts do, they are always learning things to help prepare them for their mission.

DID YOU KNOW?

Weightlessness can give some people motion sickness. This is why the plane used to train for weightlessness has the nickname the "vomit comet."

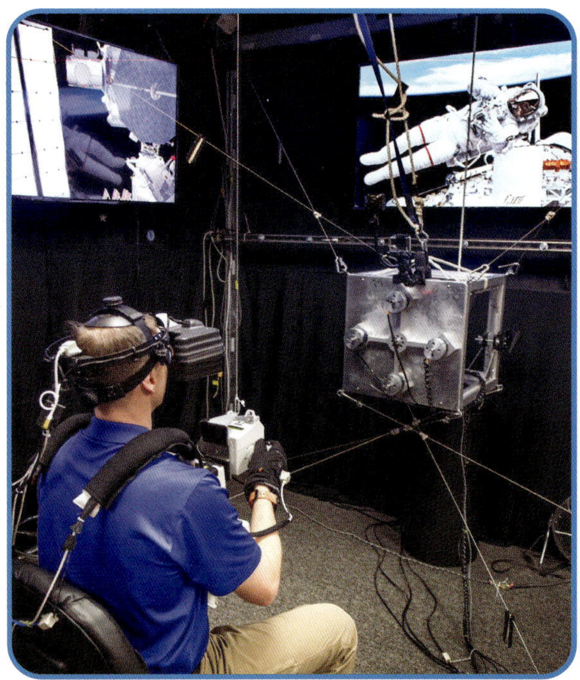

NASA astronaut Nick Hague uses a virtual reality simulator during a spacewalk emergency training.

Once an astronaut is chosen to fly on a mission to space, guess what? It's time to study more! They learn about their mission, the rocket that will launch them, and the spacecraft they'll live in. They will also learn the jobs they will have to do in space. If they will be doing science experiments, they practice them on Earth first. If they are going to take a **spacewalk**, they wear their spacesuit in the giant pool and practice using the same tools they'll use in space.

If something goes wrong or breaks, an astronaut's teachers will make them practice what to do. The more practice an astronaut has before they go to space, the safer they will be.

NASA astronaut Victor Glover descends into the pool in his Extravehicular Mobility Unit spacesuit during ISS EVA spacewalk training.

What to Pack

When astronauts are finally ready to go to space, they need to pack their bags. But what exactly should an astronaut pack? Let's think about what you and your family pack for a road trip to go camping.

Your family probably keeps some basic items in the family car in case it breaks down. The items may include a spare tire, some tools, a flashlight, and maybe some extra food and water. Astronauts have survival kits, too, in case they have a problem and land somewhere they don't expect.

These kits may include:

- food and water
- a first aid kit
- a flashlight and chemical lights
- matches
- a fishing kit
- a radio
- a life raft
- a compass and GPS

Top: Astronauts inside the International Space Station during Mission 131. Bottom: The crew of STS-124 donned pressure suits for a practice countdown before their mission began. It usually takes at least 20 minutes to put on the whole pressure suit.

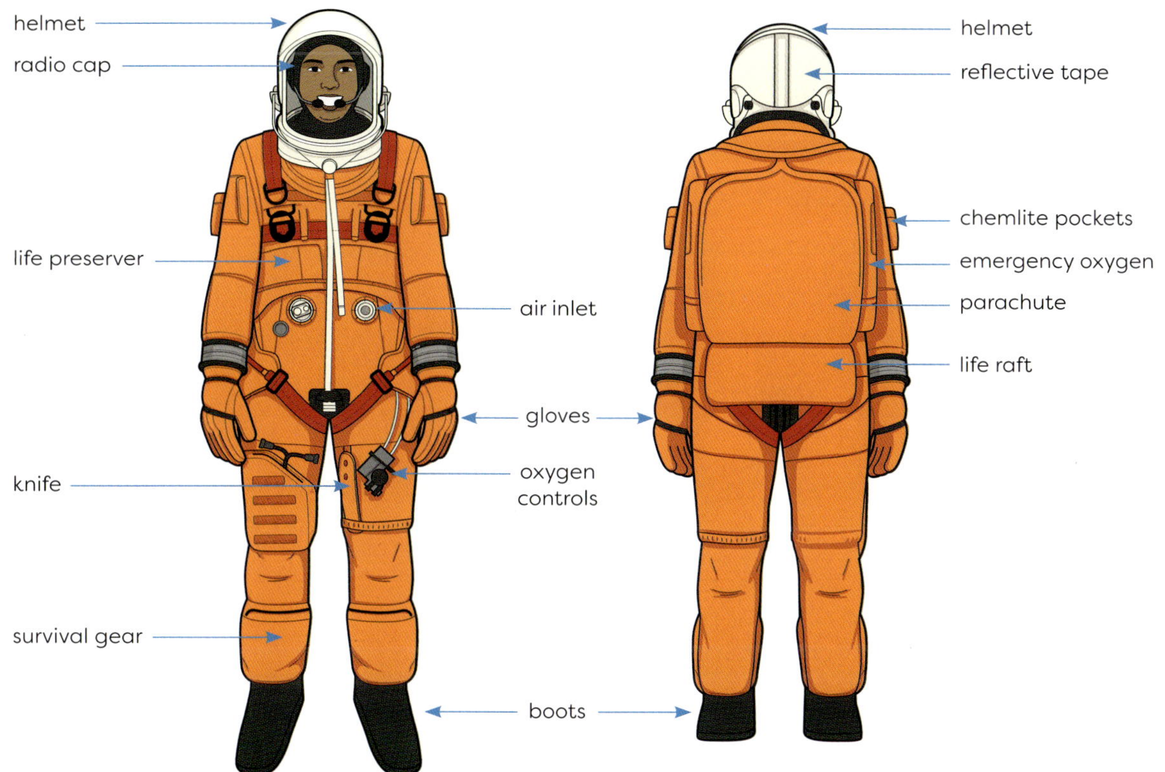

ADVANCED CREW ESCAPE SUIT (ACES)

Next, you probably make sure you have clothes for your family's camping trip. The clothes you pack probably aren't that unusual, but astronaut clothes are very special. Astronauts wear spacesuits designed for launch and landing. The suits provide oxygen in case the air leaks out of the spacecraft. They have microphones and speakers to let astronauts talk by radio with people on the ground. Astronauts have worn different launch spacesuits through the years.

Astronauts also need clothes to wear while they're in space. They don't have

EXTRAVEHICULAR MOBILITY UNIT (EMU)

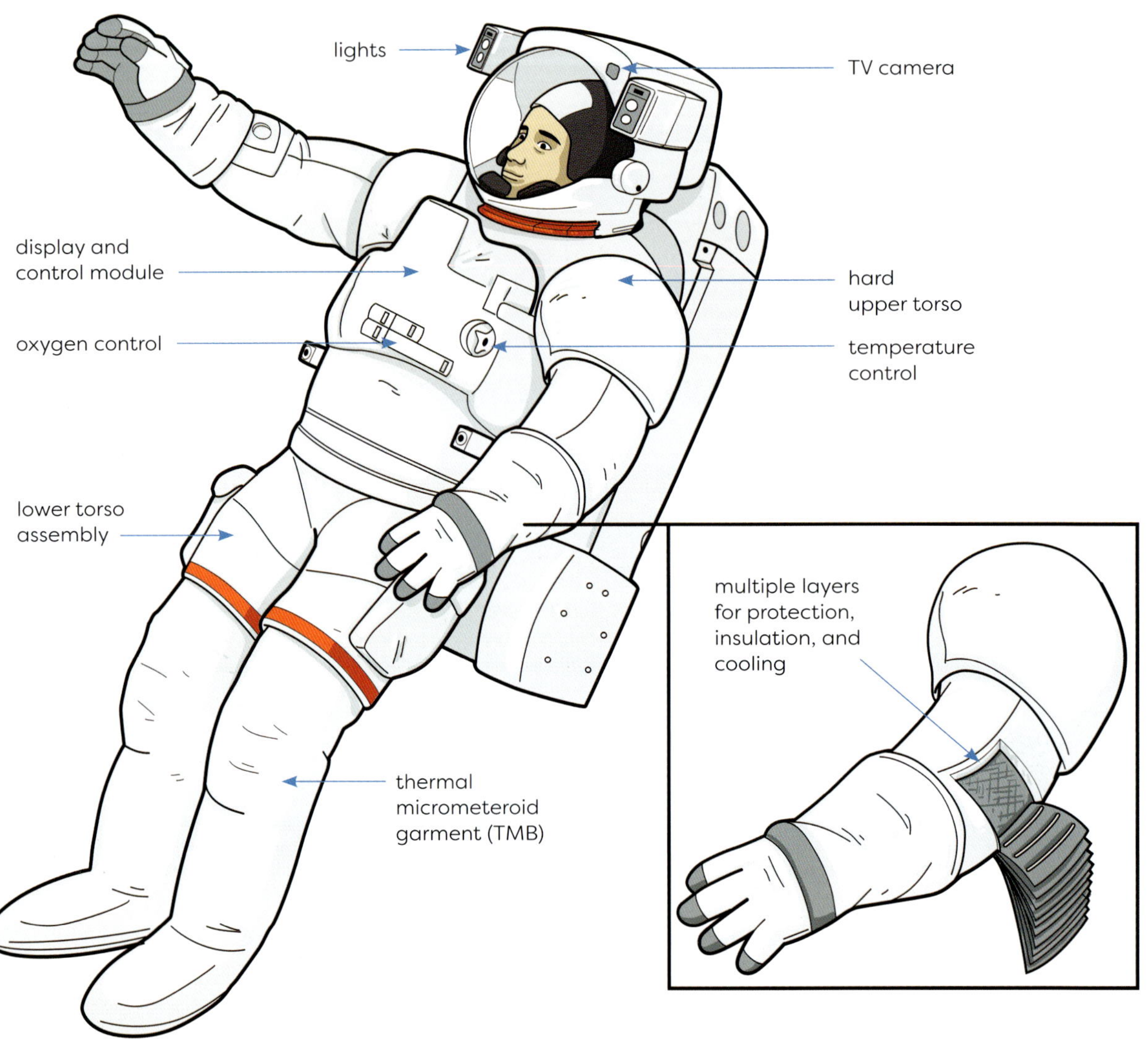

much room to pack clothes, so they often wear the same clothes for many days. The good news is that the ISS is always kept at a comfortable temperature, so they don't have to pack for cold and hot temperatures. If an astronaut needs to go outside the ISS, though, that's another story.

Astronauts need special spacesuits for going outside a spacecraft. When astronauts go outside a spacecraft, it is called a spacewalk or an **extravehicular activity (EVA)**. EVA spacesuits are different from the launch and landing suits. EVA spacesuits provide air, temperature control, and radio contact for many hours.

EVA suits have heated gloves, a special helmet, and a backpack that carries oxygen and provides electricity for the radios. The astronaut wears a cooling garment under the suit. It is covered in small tubes. Cool water is pumped through the tubes to keep the astronaut from getting too warm while working.

When your family goes on a camping trip, you may bring supplies to share with others: food and water, firewood, cooking pots, and other supplies and tools. Astronauts bring supplies to be shared in space. These include food and water, replacement parts to fix the space station, and computers. The ISS gets new supplies when new astronauts come. It also gets supplies delivered by robotic spacecraft every few weeks or months.

On the ISS, these astronauts dressed up for Halloween for fun. Clockwise from top left: Christina Koch, Luca Parmitano, Andrew Morgan and Jessica Meir.

Various robot spacecraft, like this Cygnus spacecraft, bring additional supplies to the International Space Station.

When you go on a family trip, you probably pack things that make you feel happy or things to play with. You might pack games, a stuffed buddy, or a book. Astronauts can take a few things like this into space. If they are going to the ISS, they can take up to 2.2 pounds of things in a small bag. They may bring drawings from their children, a yo-yo, or anything small that is safe on board the ISS. There are also other things like books, movies, music, or even musical instruments that can be sent to the ISS for the crew to share.

There are some things astronauts can't take to space because they might be dangerous. Things that are flammable, or burn easily, are not allowed. Astronauts also can't bring things like bread or chips. It might not seem like it, but these things are dangerous, too! They make crumbs that can float around and get stuck in air vents or machines. Anything that has a strong smell is also not allowed.

JUNIOR SCIENTISTS IN ACTION

Pack a bag to bring to space!

MATERIALS:

- **PENCIL AND PAPER OR A COMPUTER**
- **SMALL BACKPACK OR BAG**
- **SCALE**

ACTIVITY:

What would you take to space? A toy? Things to draw with? A book? Music? What else? These are not things needed to survive, but things that make you happy. Make a list of all of your choices, and be as specific as you can. Write the date down, too. This way, if you look at the list in the future, you'll know how old you were when you made it. Then you can see if your choices are different when you are older.

Now for the fun part. Astronauts can't take big or heavy items with them. Find a bag the size of a small backpack and only choose things that can fit in the bag. Once you've made your choices, take the objects out and weigh them. Does your pile weigh less than 2.2 pounds? If not, decide which objects won't be coming on the trip and weigh your things again. Repeat this until you have no more than 2.2 pounds of belongings. Was it easy or difficult to pack the things you wanted?

A Soyuz rocket carrying three people to the International Space Station in 2014.

Chapter Three

READY FOR LIFTOFF!

Once their training is complete and all their equipment is packed, an astronaut is ready to go to space. Launching a spacecraft into space is exciting, but not easy. The spacecraft has to go very fast—much faster than an airplane—to make it to space and into orbit. Rockets make this possible. Let's learn what rockets are, how they work, and about the different kinds of spacecraft they bring into orbit. Get ready for liftoff!

All About Rockets

A spacecraft cannot fly to space on its own. It needs a rocket to take it out of Earth's atmosphere. Rockets are usually tall, thin, round, and very large. **Rocket engineers** use different types of rockets to launch robotic and human spacecraft.

How do rockets work? Think about blowing up a balloon, then letting it go without tying it. The air rushes out and pushes the balloon forward. This is how rockets work. Rocket engines burn lots of **fuel** very quickly. As the fuel burns, it turns into hot gases and blows out of the back of the rocket engine through a hole. This pushes the rocket—and whatever it is attached to—forward.

You may wonder why we can't use airplanes to go to space. This is because there is no air in space. An airplane's wings need air to hold the airplane up, and its engines need air to burn fuel.

The last Space Shuttle launch (2011).

Most spacecraft are attached to the top of the rocket that brings them to space. The Space Shuttle was different. The shuttle spacecraft that held the astronauts, called an orbiter, looked like a plane with short wings. The orbiter was attached to the side of a giant fuel tank that had one large rocket on each side. When the orbiter came back from space and into the atmosphere, it used

A Soyuz rocket launch.

its wings to glide in for a landing—but it still needed rockets to get to space.

The spacecraft is only a small part of what you see on the launchpad. The rocket is the largest part, and most of the space inside it is full of fuel for the engines to burn. Rocket engines are so powerful that they can push spacecraft into space in about eight or nine minutes.

Rockets are made of two or more pieces stacked on top of each other. Each piece has its own fuel tank and engines. When a piece has used up all its fuel, it becomes useless. Its weight slows down the rocket. Think of running while pulling a heavy sled behind you. You will go faster if you let go of the sled. The same is true for a rocket going to space. As each piece is used up, it detaches from the rocket. Most of these rocket pieces are destroyed on the way down, but some rockets have pieces that can be used again.

Rockets are used to launch many kinds of robotic spacecraft. Many of these spacecraft are designed to orbit the Earth. They are called **satellites**. There are thousands of satellites orbiting the Earth right now. There are satellites for weather, TV, phones, and many other uses.

Rockets also launch spacecraft that leave Earth's orbit to study our solar system. Some fly by other planets and record what they see. Others orbit around planets or moons for months or years. Atmospheric **probes** explore the atmospheres of other planets. Robotic spacecraft landers check out things on the surface. Rovers actually drive on other planets or moons.

DID YOU KNOW?

The Saturn V rocket that launched Apollo 12 was struck twice by lightning in the first minute after liftoff. The spacecraft was not harmed and successfully made it to the Moon.

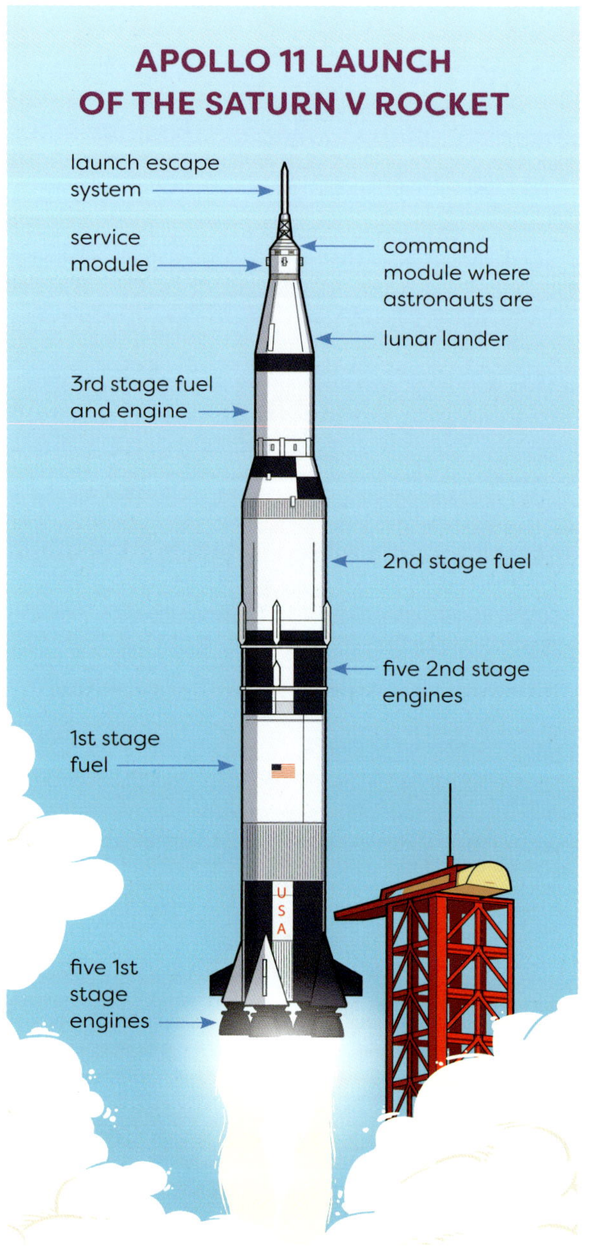

Crewed Spacecraft

Crewed spacecraft are much bigger than robotic spacecraft. They must carry all the things people in the crew need to stay alive, including air, food, water, and temperature controls. Because crewed spacecraft are so big and heavy, very large rockets are used to launch them.

Crewed spacecraft must be designed to safely bring astronauts back to Earth. Spacecraft in orbit are going superfast. When a spacecraft enters Earth's atmosphere, air rushes past it. The **friction** of the air makes the spacecraft's surface extremely hot. These spacecraft must

Inside their Soyuz spacecraft (from left), Paolo Nespoli, Sergey Ryazanskiy and Randy Bresnik are shown preparing to return to Earth from the ISS. They are wearing their Sokol launch and entry suits.

have **heat shields** that protect the astronauts and the rest of the spacecraft from the heat. Robotic spacecraft usually don't have heat shields. When they come back into the atmosphere, they break apart and burn up.

Astronaut John Glenn with his Mercury spacecraft. Glenn in this spacecraft was the first American to orbit the Earth in 1962. The spacecraft was just big enough for one person.

There have been many different robotic spacecraft, but only a few types of crewed spacecraft. The Soviet Union sent Yuri Gagarin to space in a small spacecraft that fit only one person. It was called the Vostok spacecraft. The first American in space also flew in a one-person spacecraft. It was called the Mercury spacecraft. Later, the United States used the two-person Gemini spacecraft. The Soviets moved to the three-person Voskhod.

When America sent astronauts to the Moon, it used an Apollo

A DEEPER LOOK

If you turn off an airplane's engines, it will gradually slow to a stop. What happens when you turn off a spacecraft's rocket engine in space? It doesn't stop! There is no air to slow down the spacecraft. Once in space, a spacecraft usually coasts with its rocket engines off. Astronauts only turn on the engines for short amounts of time to change the shape of their orbit.

The Apollo 11 Lunar Module on the surface of the Moon. Astronaut Buzz Aldrin is in front of the lander.

A Soyuz spacecraft approaching its docking port.

A Space Shuttle about to land after a mission in space.

three-person spacecraft. The Apollo spacecraft had three pieces. One part contained the rocket that took the spacecraft to the Moon and back. The Lunar Module took two astronauts to the Moon's surface. While the two astronauts were on the Moon, the Command Module was home for the third astronaut. The Command Module also returned the three astronauts to Earth. So far, Apollo is the only spacecraft that has taken humans to the Moon.

DID YOU KNOW?

The Apollo missions brought back 842 pounds of moon rocks and dirt to Earth. That is about the weight of five adults!

The Soviets built the Soyuz spacecraft in the 1960s. A type of Soyuz is still being used today to take people to and from the ISS. This spacecraft can hold three astronauts.

The United States flew Space Shuttle spacecraft from 1981 to 2011. Each of the five shuttles could hold seven astronauts. The shuttles were used to take satellites into orbit, to bring astronauts and equipment to the ISS, and for many experiments.

China built a three-person spacecraft called Shenzhou. It is like the Soyuz but a little bigger.

New spacecraft are being designed right now. The future of space travel is exciting!

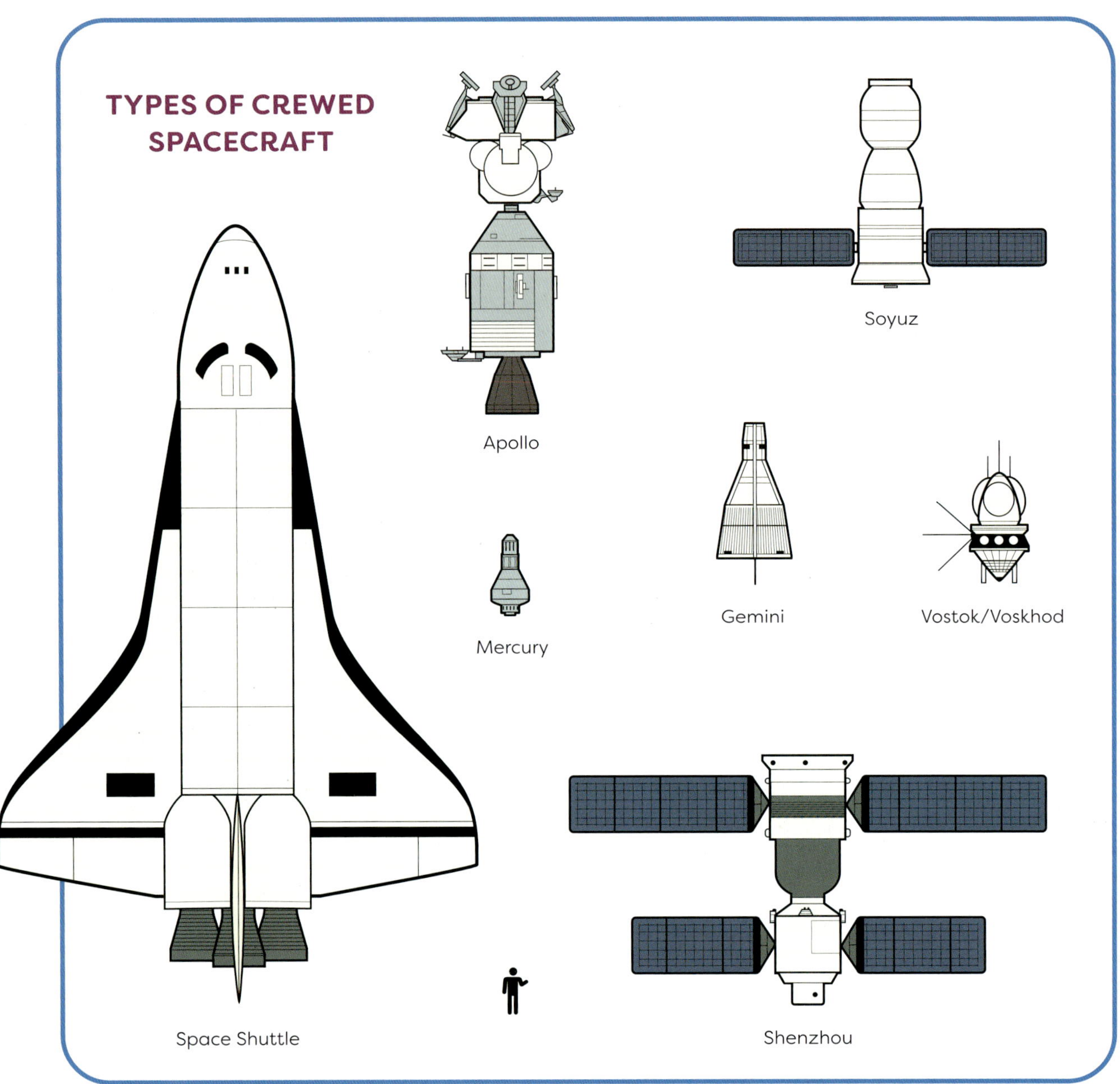
TYPES OF CREWED SPACECRAFT
Apollo
Soyuz
Mercury
Gemini
Vostok/Voskhod
Space Shuttle
Shenzhou

SPACEWALKING

Astronaut Stephen Robinson performs an EVA attached to the ISS robot arm.

There is often work that needs to be done outside a spacecraft or the ISS. For those jobs, astronauts need to go on an EVA ("extravehicular activity," remember?). An astronaut may spacewalk to work on a satellite, to test new equipment, or to fix things that are broken outside their spacecraft. Parts of the International Space Station were even built by spacewalking astronauts!

Any time an astronaut goes on an EVA, there is some danger—but they take many steps to put safety first! They not only practice EVAs before going to space, but they also stay in contact with other astronauts in the spacecraft the whole time. When an astronaut goes on an EVA at the ISS, they are attached to the station at all times.

JUNIOR SCIENTISTS IN ACTION

Design your very own rocket!

MATERIALS:

PAPER

PENCIL

CRAYONS OR COLORED PENCILS

RULER (OPTIONAL)

ACTIVITY:

Pretend you are a rocket engineer. How would you design a rocket that could carry humans into space? Take a look at some of the pictures of rockets in this book to get some ideas. Do you want your rocket to look like one of them, or a mix of more than one type? Read and answer the questions below. They will help you come up with a design.

- Will your rocket be long and skinny, or will it have a different shape, like the Space Shuttle?
- Design the spacecraft that will actually carry humans. What does it look like?
- Where will the spacecraft be on the rocket?
- Where will the fuel tanks be?
- How many engines will the rocket have?

- What color or colors will the rocket be? Will it have words or symbols on it?
- What will you name your rocket?

When you have answers to all of these questions, draw your design on a piece of paper. You can use a ruler to draw straight lines if you like. Color your final design. Then name your rocket and sign your drawing with today's date. Good job!

If you want to try to build a model of your rocket, paper towel and toilet paper tubes make great model rockets! Use paint or construction paper to cover them and add fun features!

On board the ISS, Christina Koch poses with Andrew Morgan and Nick Hague, who are suited up in their EVA spacesuits and ready to go outside into space.

Chapter Four

LIFE IN SPACE

So, what is it like to actually live in space? We've learned how space is different from Earth. In many ways, life in space is also the same as life on Earth. To begin with, you need a home. In space, it could be a spacecraft or a space station. You also need to eat, drink, sleep, use the bathroom, bathe, work, exercise, and find ways to have fun. Many of these things are not done in quite the same way in space as on your home planet. Let's see what life is like in space!

Your Home

These days, home sweet home for astronauts is usually a space station. In the past, astronauts lived in the spacecraft that took them into space. Those spacecraft were small and cramped, so the missions couldn't last very long. Now, most astronauts travel to space in one spacecraft, then live in the International Space Station.

The ISS is the largest space station ever built. It is also the only one still in orbit. The first piece was launched into space in 1998. Many more pieces have been added over many years. Five different space agencies helped build and improve the station: those of Russia, the United States, Japan, Europe, and Canada.

The International Space Station has most of the things you probably have in your home; it's just not as comfy. It has places to eat, sleep, exercise and hang

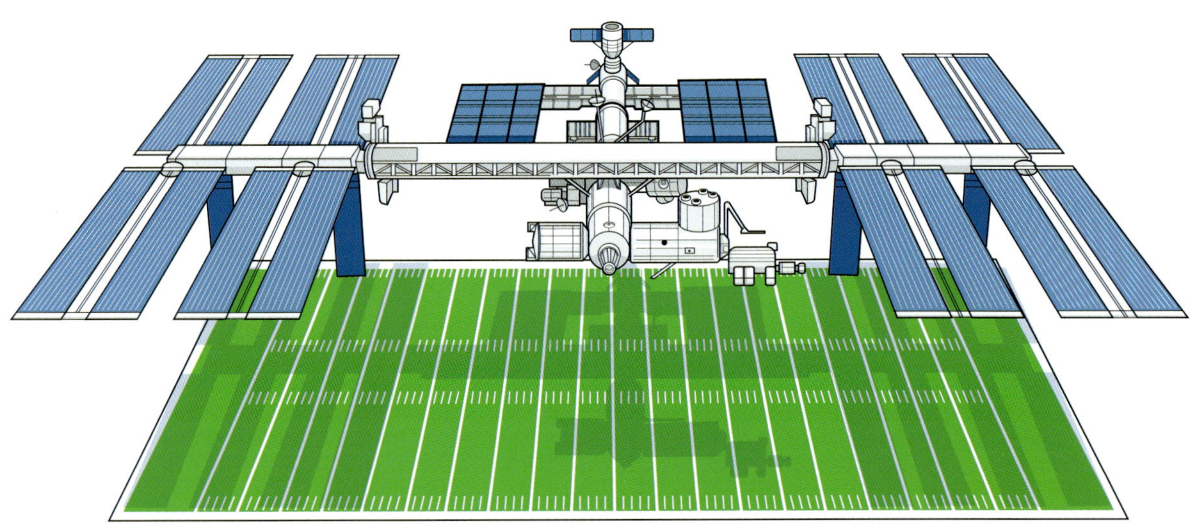

The International Space Station is about the size of a football field.

out—plus windows so astronauts can watch the Earth go by. The ISS also has a work area where astronauts can do their science experiments.

Once an astronaut is on board the ISS, they usually stay for a few months. They share the space with two to five other astronauts. The ISS has not been empty of people since the year 2000. Since it opened, the ISS has had 240 visitors from 19 countries!

The ISS looks like it has four pairs of flat "wings." These are very large solar panels that turn the Sun's light into energy. That energy is used to power the lights, computers, machines, and other electronics. Solar panels used on Earth do the same thing.

If you live in a house, you may have a garage that can hold one or more cars. The space station has **docking ports**. Docking ports are where the astronauts' spacecraft attach to the space station so they can go inside. The ISS has six docking ports. This means that six spacecraft can be attached to it at the same time.

DID YOU KNOW?

Sometimes you can spot the ISS from your own backyard! It looks like a very bright star moving across the night sky. We can see it because sunlight reflects off of the ISS's solar panels and the rest of the station. Check out the More to Explore section in the back of the book (page 72) to find out when and where to look for it!

Your Job

So, what do astronauts actually do while they are in space? They work! Astronauts have jobs to do. While on the International Space Station, they spend a lot of time doing science experiments.

Some astronauts study how space affects the human body. They run medical experiments on themselves. These experiments have told us that people's bodies change in space. For example, space travel makes bones and muscles weaker. Other experiments have proved that exercising in space helps keep bones and muscles healthy, so exercise is very important for astronauts.

Astronauts experiment with animals and plants to test their reactions to **microgravity**, another word for why people and objects appear to be weightless in space. Astronauts have studied everything from lettuce and spiders to fish and microbes, which are microscopic living things. Scientists find that most life does pretty well in space.

On the ISS, Leroy Chiao performs an ultrasound examination on the eye of Salizhan Sharipov.

DID YOU KNOW?
Astronauts are taller in space! Their "padding" between the bones in their backs stretches out without gravity.

Astronauts also study other materials. For example, astronauts have grown

Jessica Meir cuts mizuna mustard green leaves grown on the ISS, part of research on how to provide fresh food to crews on long-duration missions.

nearly perfect crystals in microgravity. They have also looked at how small flames act in the space station. Believe it or not, flames are round in space!

Just like houses on Earth, the International Space Station needs to be taken care of. The crew on the ISS makes sure it stays in good shape. They clean it, check equipment, and fix or replace things that break. Sometimes things need to be fixed outside of the ISS. That's when it's time for a spacewalk!

Astronauts may also take pictures of the Earth as part of their job. Some of the pictures are used to study Earth. Others are just for fun!

When the Space Shuttles were still flying, they had missions to put satellites in space. Sometimes a shuttle was sent to grab satellites already in orbit for repairs or to bring them back to Earth. The

Space Shuttle Discovery took the Hubble Space Telescope into space in 1990. The Hubble is still orbiting the Earth today!

Part of every astronaut's job is to talk with people working on the mission from the ground. It's important for people on Earth to know what the astronauts are doing. Hundreds of people on the ground are there to support and direct astronauts in space.

Astronauts Mark C. Lee (left) and Steven L. Smith conduct an EVA to service the Hubble Space Telescope.

Soichi Noguchi uses a camera at a window in the cupola (a set of windows) of the ISS with China in the background.

Your Daily Life

What is it like to do things such as eat, sleep, use the bathroom, exercise, and take baths in space? These things are pretty simple on Earth, but astronauts need to do them while floating in microgravity.

Let's talk about food. The first astronauts squeezed edible goo out of tubes—almost like baby food. That food was nutritious, but not very tasty. These days, astronaut food is much more like food on Earth. The ISS is stocked with packaged foods that last a long time. Most of the food is already cooked, so it is either ready to eat or can be heated in a small warming oven. Some food is dehydrated. This means the water has been removed. Astronauts add water, heat, then eat! When spacecraft arrive at the ISS, they bring fresh foods like fruit.

DID YOU KNOW?
The ISS doesn't have a freezer, refrigerator, stove, or microwave—just a small warming oven.

Peggy Whitson (left) and Valery Korzun, eating on the ISS. A tomato and hamburgers are floating.

What about sleeping? There are no beds on the ISS. Instead, astronauts often sleep inside bags that are attached to a wall so they don't float around the cabin while napping. Astronauts on the ISS have a small, closet-like space where they can sleep, watch movies on a computer, or read. Astronauts are able to email people on Earth. They can even call their families. Some astronauts like to post things on social media about their experiences in space.

When astronauts first started going to space, there were no bathrooms. Astronauts used bags instead! *Ew!* Today, the ISS has two bathrooms. Astronauts strap themselves to the toilet seat. When they are finished, the space toilet uses suction instead of water to "flush" the waste.

What about washing? Instead of showering or taking a bath, astronauts use wet towels to wipe themselves clean. To wash their hair, astronauts can use a tiny bit of water and no-rinse shampoo. They have to be careful not to let drops of water escape into the air so they don't get into any electronics or machines and damage them.

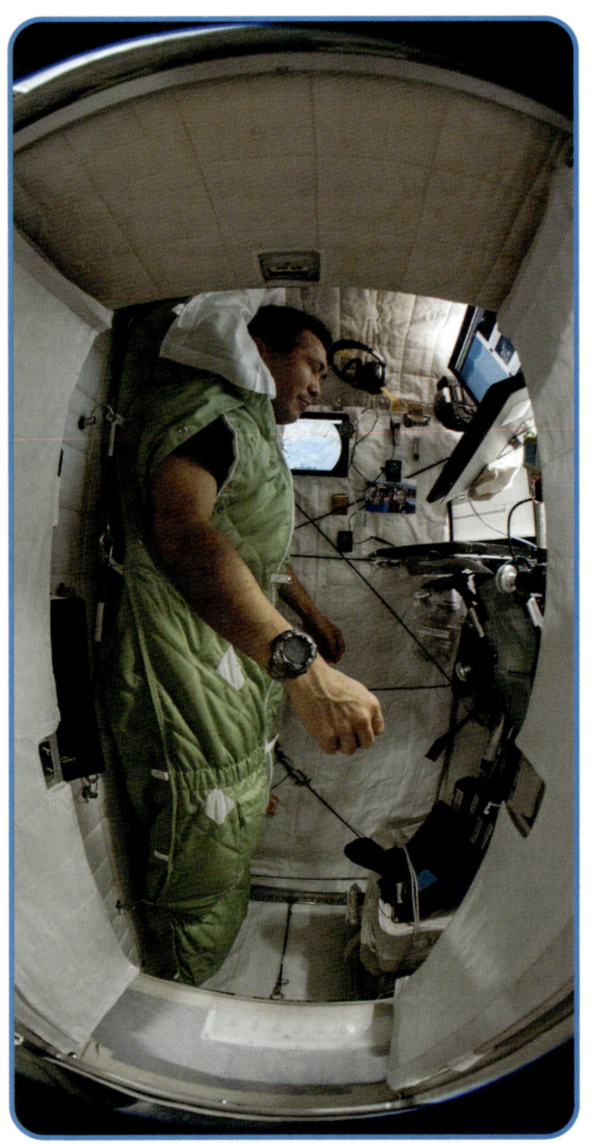

Koichi Wakata, strapped into his sleeping bag in his sleep station where he can sleep, watch movies or use the laptop.

DID YOU KNOW?

Astronauts wear adult diapers on their trips to and from the ISS or while doing EVAs for several hours. Really!

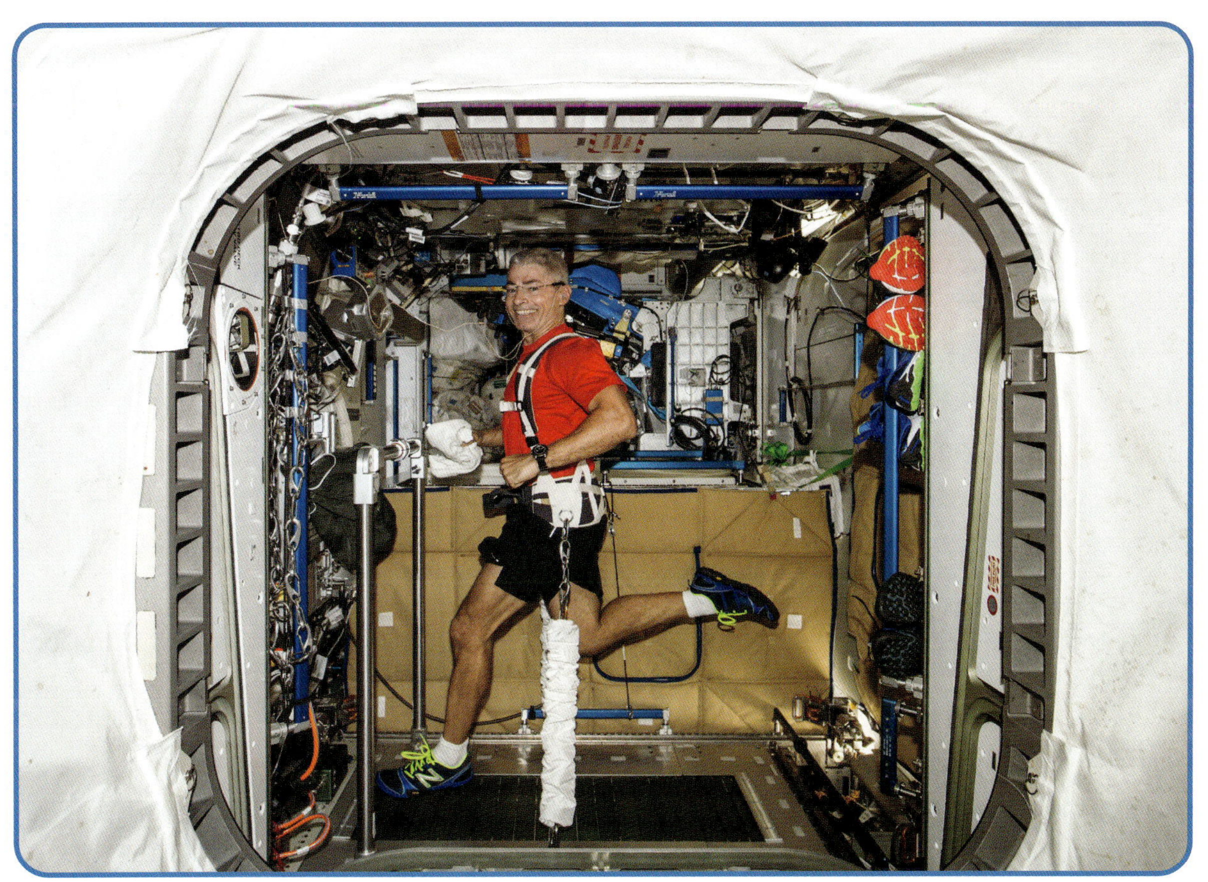

Astronaut Mark Vande Hei exercises on the COLBERT treadmill aboard the International Space Station.

ISS astronauts must exercise for two hours every day to keep their muscles and bones strong. They use a treadmill with straps to keep them from flying off the machine. Instead of lifting weights (which would not have any weight in microgravity), astronauts use stretchy straps and machines to build muscle.

Astronauts often have motion sickness the first few days in space. After that time, their bodies adjust, and they feel fine.

JUNIOR SCIENTISTS IN ACTION

Astronauts use something called a glove box on the ISS to do some experiments. The box is used to protect the astronaut from dangerous materials and to protect the experiment inside from dust, dirt, or germs. It can be hard to do things inside a glove box. Let's see what it's like to use one!

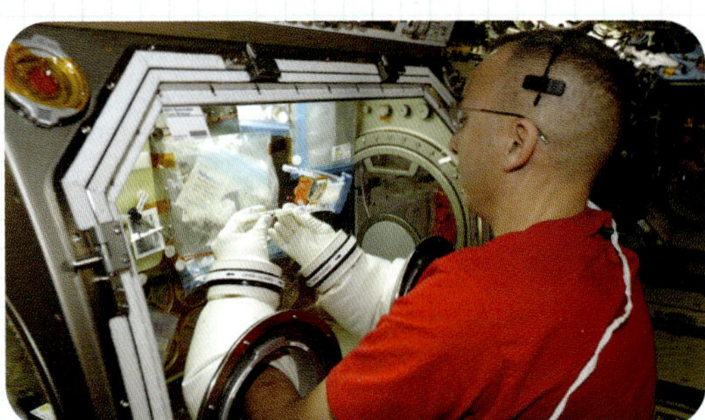

Astronaut Randy Bresnik uses a glove box while working on a cancer research experiment aboard the International Space Station.

BE SAFE! Have an adult help you with this activity.

MATERIALS:

- SCISSORS
- MEDIUM CARDBOARD BOX
- SMALL RUBBER GLOVES (DISHWASHING GLOVES ARE FINE)
- DUCT TAPE
- PIECE OF PAPER
- PENCIL OR CRAYON
- CLEAR PLASTIC WRAP

ACTIVITY:

1. Ask an adult to cut off the top flaps of the box.
2. Then ask an adult to cut two holes in one side of the box. The

holes should be large enough to put your hands through.

3. Push one glove through each hole so that the finger sections are inside the box.
4. Use duct tape to attach the wrist of each glove to the outside of the holes. Be sure to leave room in the opening of the glove for your hand.
5. Put the paper and the pencil into the glove box.
6. Cover the top of the box with plastic wrap and tape it in place.
7. Place your hands in the gloves. You are ready to experiment!

Can you fold a piece of paper? Write your name? What else could you try?

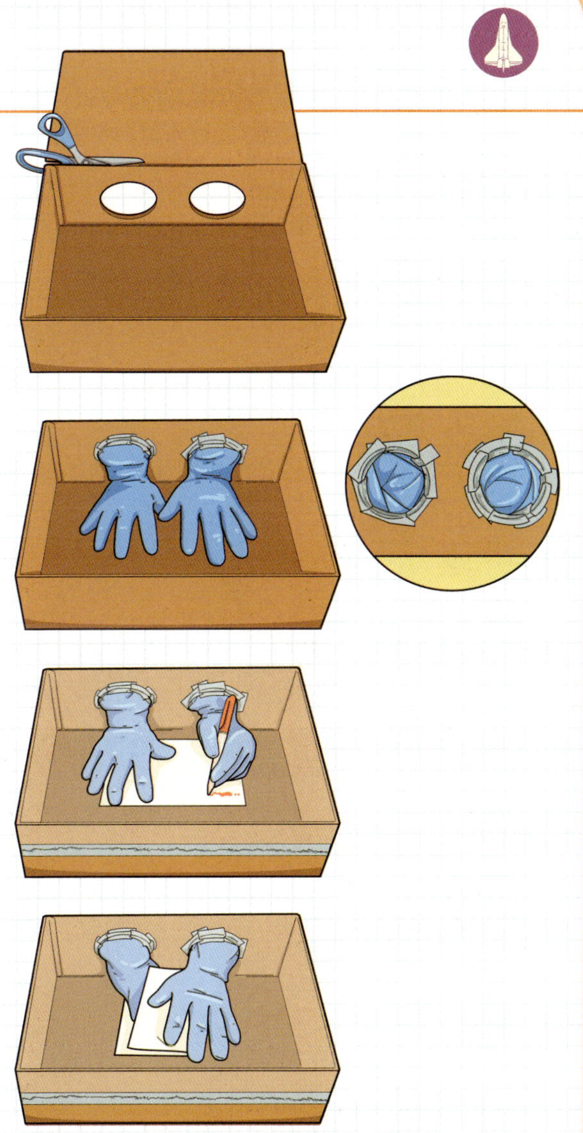

The Lunar Rover of Apollo 17 on the Moon.
Astronaut Gene Cernan is driving.

Chapter Five

WHO (AND WHAT) HAS BEEN TO SPACE?

About one hundred billion (100,000,000,000) people throughout history have lived on Earth. How many have been to space? Fewer than 600!

People from more than 40 countries have been to space, but only three countries have launched people into space: the Soviet Union/Russia, the United States, and China. Most astronauts have been Americans and Soviets/Russians. In this chapter, we'll learn about some of the amazing things astronauts have done. We'll also talk about animals and some odd things that have gone to space.

Famous Firsts and Fantastic Feats

Sending humans to space was a big accomplishment. The astronauts who traveled to space have done incredible things. Let's explore some of the famous firsts and fantastic feats of these courageous space explorers.

FIRST HUMAN IN SPACE (1961):

Yuri Gagarin. He orbited the Earth once in his Vostok 1 spacecraft.

DID YOU KNOW?
Gagarin's spacecraft was not designed to land a human safely. Once he was low enough in Earth's atmosphere, Gagarin left the Vostok 1 and parachuted down to Earth.

FIRST AMERICAN IN SPACE (1961):

Alan Shepard Jr. He flew a **sub-orbital flight**. This means he went up to space, then came down, but did not orbit.

FIRST AMERICAN TO ORBIT THE EARTH (1962):

John Glenn. He orbited Earth three times in the Friendship 7 spacecraft.

FIRST WOMAN IN SPACE (1963):

Valentina Tereshkova. She was in space for almost three days and orbited Earth 48 times in Vostok 6.

FIRST SPACEWALK (1963):

Alexei Leonov. His spacewalk lasted about 12 minutes.

FIRST AMERICAN SPACEWALK (1965):

Ed White. He was outside his spacecraft for 23 minutes, attached by a 25-foot lifeline.

FIRST HUMANS TO WALK ON THE MOON (1969):

Neil Armstrong and Buzz Aldrin. When Armstrong first set foot on the moon, he said, "That's one small step for a man, one giant leap for mankind."

FIRST TIME HUMANS DROVE ON THE MOON (1971):

Apollo 15 astronauts took a **lunar rover** for a spin on the Moon's surface. They said it was a bouncy, exciting ride.

FIRST LATIN AMERICAN PERSON IN SPACE (1980):

Arnaldo Tamayo Méndez. He flew on a Soyuz mission to the Salyut 6 space station.

FIRST AMERICAN WOMAN IN SPACE (1983):

Sally Ride. She traveled on a Space Shuttle Challenger mission that put satellites in space.

FIRST AFRICAN AMERICAN IN SPACE (1983):

Guion Bluford Jr. He was on a Space Shuttle Challenger mission that put a satellite in space, and completed many experiments.

FIRST SPACEWALK WITHOUT BEING ATTACHED TO A SPACECRAFT (1984):

Bruce McCandless II. He used a special "backpack" to move through space outside the Space Shuttle Challenger.

FIRST ASIAN AMERICAN IN SPACE (1985):

Ellison Onizuka. He traveled on a Space Shuttle Discovery flight that put a satellite into orbit.

FIRST AFRICAN AMERICAN WOMAN IN SPACE (1992):

Mae Jemison. She flew on the Space Shuttle Endeavour on a shuttle flight and did experiments with human bone cells.

FIRST AND ONLY THREE-PERSON SPACEWALK (1992):

Three Space Shuttle Endeavour astronauts grabbed a huge satellite by hand and attached it to the shuttle to be repaired.

LONGEST SINGLE TRIP TO SPACE:

Valeri Polyakov spent 438 days (about one year and two months) in space on a Mir space-station flight.

OLDEST PERSON TO FLY IN SPACE:

John Glenn. He took his last trip into space when he was 77 years old.

FIRST ASTRONAUTS TO STAY ON BOARD THE INTERNATIONAL SPACE STATION (2000):

Yuri Gidzenko, Bill Shepherd, and Sergei Krikalev. More than 240 astronauts have stayed on the ISS, in groups of three to six at a time, since then.

LONGEST SPACEWALK (2001):

James Voss and Susan Helms. They spent almost nine hours doing ISS construction in their EVA suits.

FIRST TOURIST IN SPACE (2001):

Dennis Tito. He paid the Russian space program 20 million dollars ($20,000,000) to fly to the ISS for a few days.

MOST TIME IN SPACE TOTAL:

Gennady Padalka. He spent 879 days (about two years and five months) in space during five different stays on Mir and the ISS.

MOST TIME IN SPACE BY AN AMERICAN AND BY A WOMAN:

Peggy A. Whitson. She has spent 665 days (about 1 year and 10 months) during her three stays on the ISS.

Animals in Space

Did you know that humans weren't the first living creatures to go to space? Scientists weren't sure that space would be safe for humans, so they sent animals first to test how spaceflight affected them.

The first animals to leave Earth's atmosphere were fruit flies in 1947. They went up to space for a few minutes, then came back down, without going into orbit.

In 1957, the Soviet Union sent their first animal into orbit—a stray dog named Laika that flew on Sputnik 2. Later, Russia sent two dogs named Veterok and Ugolyok into space. They orbited the Earth for 22 days.

The first animals to fly around the Moon were two tortoises and some fruit flies aboard Zond 5 in 1968. Some Apollo missions carried living things to the Moon and back, including microscopic creatures, plant seeds, and even mice.

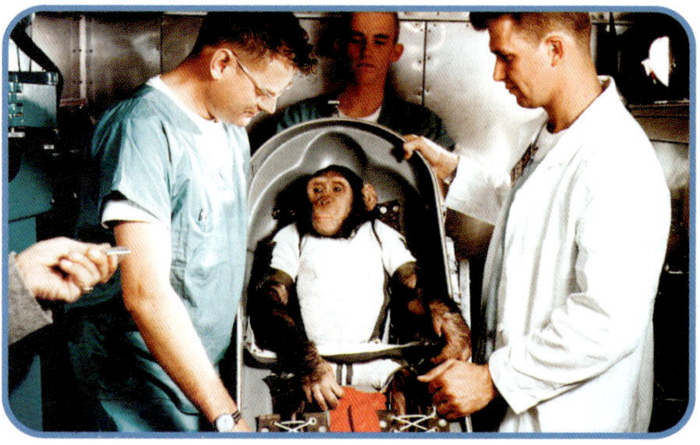

A chimpanzee, named Ham, in the biopack couch for the MR-2 suborbital test flight. While on his flight, Ham performed lever-pulling tasks in response to flashing lights.

A spider spun a web in space on Skylab in 1973. At first it was confused, but then it figured it out.

Since then, bullfrogs, spiders, ants, and even newts have made the trip to space. Today, astronauts often take plants and animals to the International Space Station for study.

Weird Stuff in Space

If you went to space, you might bring a toy. Astronauts like toys, too! A Buzz Lightyear toy spent 467 days on the ISS—a longer visit than any person. A Smokey Bear stuffed toy also spent time on the ISS.

Aluminum LEGO bricks have gone to the surface of Mars on robotic spacecraft. LEGO minifigures are orbiting Jupiter on the Juno spacecraft.

Items from history have made history again by going to space. Parts of the first airplane, the *Wright Flyer,* flew on various missions, including Apollo 11. Luke Skywalker's lightsaber from the movie *Return of the Jedi* also flew to space and back.

In 2018, SpaceX tested its Falcon Heavy rocket. It carried a real car with a fake astronaut, named Starman, in it. The car—and Starman—are still in space today!

In 2012, Smokey Bear floats freely in the hatchway of the International Space Station's Destiny laboratory.

The mannequin known as "Starman," seated in the Roadster car with the Earth in the background. The car and mannequin launched on the first Falcon Heavy rocket.

VOYAGER GOLDEN RECORD

A picture of one of the gold-plated copper records included on Voyager 1 and Voyager 2.

One of the biggest questions astronomers have is whether or not there is life on other planets or around other stars. Life beyond Earth, called extraterrestrial life, may exist, but so far we haven't found any. We now know that there are a lot of stars and planets in the universe. So, there may be life, even intelligent "aliens." If there are aliens, they are likely to be extremely far away.

If we wanted to send a message to extraterrestrials, what would it say? Scientists thought about that question before launching the Voyager 1 and 2 spacecraft in 1977. Both Voyagers are now in interstellar space—the space between our Sun and the next-closest stars. Each Voyager spacecraft carries a Golden Record. The record is a disc covered in gold that has messages and information from Earth for any aliens that might find the spacecraft far in the future. How far? It will take the Voyagers tens of thousands of years to get near other stars!

Each record is a time capsule with information about our world and the people that live here. What will the aliens find on the record? There are pictures of humans, plants, animals, cars, and cities. Some pictures show people in different cultures doing everyday things. Scientists included scientific drawings and even photos of planets in our solar system. There are also many sounds, including greetings in many languages, singing, nature sounds, and music from all over the world!

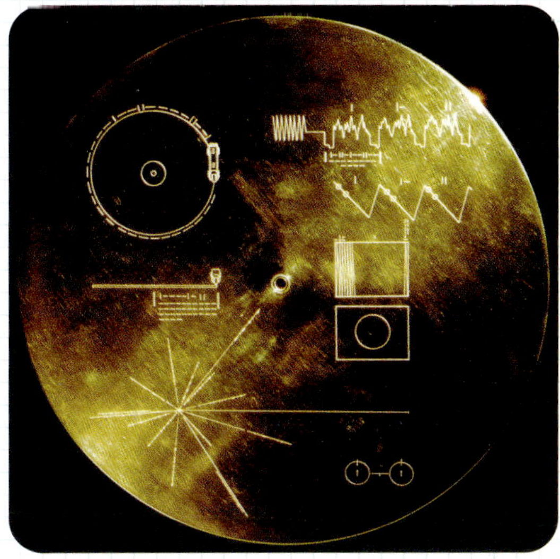

The cover of the Voyager record protects the record from micrometeorite bombardment, and also provides information for how to play the record.

JUNIOR SCIENTISTS IN ACTION

What would you send to space for aliens to find? Let's make a list!

MATERIALS:

PENCIL AND PAPER OR A COMPUTER

ACTIVITY:

What things would you include on your version of a Golden Record? You can include pictures and sounds. Write things down on a piece of paper, in a notebook, or with a computer. Here are some questions that might help you make your list:

Would you include pictures of people, animals, places, or something else? Make sure your answers are specific—what people would you include? What kinds of animals?

What songs or types of music would you choose to include?

Are there other sounds you think aliens would find interesting? What are they?

The Golden Records have greetings from people around the world. What would your greeting say? Who would you ask to record a greeting for your record?

Make sure you write down the date of your list. Then you can look back at your ideas

in the future and think about whether you would change anything on the list.

Another thing you can do is make a time capsule with some of the things you selected. You can put photos and drawings in a box, or you could use a computer to make a digital time capsule and put photos, sounds, and songs on a USB flash drive. Keep the box or USB drive somewhere safe so you can open your own time capsule years from now.

Astronauts standing behind their launch entry suits.

Chapter Six

YOUR TICKET TO SPACE

Now that you've learned all about what it takes to be an astronaut, maybe you think you'd like to be one someday. That's great! You are never too young to start preparing for a future job as an astronaut.

What Can You Do Now?

There are many ways for you to learn about space exploration—and have fun doing it! This book was a great start, and there are many other great books out there. Ask a parent to help you find space sites on the Internet, or look for videos online or at your local library. You can always check out the NASA website to see what astronauts on the space station are doing right now. The More to Explore section in the back of this book (page 72) lists some other good sites to visit.

Want some hands-on space experiences? See if you can visit a local planetarium or space-related museum. You might even be able to attend a space camp.

Are you excited about what you've learned so far? You can be a space teacher for family and friends. You can start by sharing what you've read in this book.

Make sure you check out the night sky! Learn how to find the ISS or locate other planets. Find out when the next meteor shower is and maybe you'll see some meteors!

Whatever you choose to do, I hope you will continue to enjoy learning about space exploration.

What Can You Do in the Future?

To become a US astronaut, you need to go to college to study a STEM field (Science, Technology, Engineering, or Math). Then you must work in one of those fields or have experience as a jet pilot. Make sure you exercise! You will need to be in good shape and be able to pass a lot of medical exams. When you are older, you can learn more about the things you need to do. For now, enjoy learning about space, doing well in school, and staying physically fit.

In the ISS, the Space Shuttle STS-131 crew members and ISS Expedition 23 crew members combine to make 13 happy astronauts in space.

Make sure you do things because you like doing them—not just because you think they will help you become an astronaut. Thousands of people do everything they need to do to get into the astronaut program, but only 10 or 20 are selected each year. It is hard to become an astronaut, but if you find a job you enjoy, you'll be happy whether you are selected to be an astronaut or not.

Remember that there are all sorts of jobs in space exploration. Besides astronauts, scientists, and engineers, there are also writers, artists, managers, and people doing many other jobs. So, as you can see, the sky is the limit when it comes to working in the space exploration field.

For now, your job is just to have fun learning! Enjoy!

Humans first walked on the Moon during the Apollo 11 mission. Neil Armstrong took the first steps.

GLOSSARY

astronaut: A person who is trained to travel in space

astronomer: A person who studies everything outside of Earth's atmosphere, often using telescopes

atmosphere: The gases surrounding a planet, moon, or other object in space

cosmonaut: A Soviet or Russian astronaut

crewed spacecraft: A spacecraft that carries humans to space

docking port: Where one spacecraft can attach to another spacecraft or space station

extravehicular activity (EVA): Anything an astronaut does outside a spacecraft while wearing a spacesuit (also called a spacewalk)

friction: The force caused by two objects sliding against each other that makes them slow down or stop

fuel: Something that is burned to make heat or power

gravity: The force that keeps you on the ground

heat shields: Parts of some spacecraft that protect the inside of the spacecraft from heat caused by entering the atmosphere

launch: The process of sending something into space

lunar rover: A special vehicle that is made to drive on the Moon

microgravity: When people or objects appear to be weightless and float

orbit: The path that a spacecraft, moon, or other object follows as it goes around another object

planet: A big, round, ball-shaped mass that goes around the Sun (but not around another object) and does not have anything close to the same size near its orbit

probe: A robotic spacecraft that is sent into space to get information about a planet, asteroid, moon, or other space object

robotic spacecraft: A spacecraft that does not have any people on it and is controlled by computers or people on Earth

rocket: A vehicle that takes a spacecraft into space, or a type of engine that burns fuel and pushes hot gases out of an opening to make an object move forward

rocket engineer: A person who designs, builds, and tests machines that can fly—including rockets, satellites, and spacecraft

satellite: An object that orbits a larger object

solar system: A group of planets and objects that revolve, or go around, a star

spacecraft: A vehicle or vehicles designed to fly in space

space station: A spacecraft in orbit where astronauts can live for a long time

spacesuit: Special clothing that has everything an astronaut needs to survive outside a spacecraft, including air

spacewalk: Anything an astronaut does outside a spacecraft while wearing a spacesuit (also called an EVA)

sub-orbital flight: When a spacecraft goes to space and then comes right back down without going all the way around the Earth

telescope: A scientific tool that makes far-away objects appear closer

MORE TO EXPLORE

NASA Kids' Club:
NASA.gov/kidsclub/index.html. Visit this page for games and information about NASA.

NASA Space Place:
SpacePlace.NASA.gov. This website, designed for kids, lets visitors learn about space and enjoy space-related activities, experiments, and crafts.

NASA's Spot the Station:
SpotTheStation.NASA.gov. Find out when you can see the ISS fly over your location. Make sure you enter your city!

Random Space Facts:
RandomSpaceFact.com. This is the author's website that offers information about the author and links to his other astronomy-related content, including videos, a radio show, classes, and social media accounts.

Check out the author's other children's space books, including *Astronomy for Kids* and *Super Cool Space Facts*.

INDEX

ACKNOWLEDGMENTS

Thanks to Jennifer Vaughn for her guidance, love, and support, and to my sons, Kevin and Daniel Betts, for their support and for bringing happiness and fulfillment to my life. Thanks to my parents, Bert A. and Barbara Lang Betts, for supporting my interest in space. Thanks to Kathleen Reagan Betts for being such a great mom. And thanks to Bill Nye and the staff of The Planetary Society for their support of my broader education efforts. Thanks to my editor, Aarti Kelapure, for making this a better book, and to Susan Haynes and the rest of the Callisto Media team.

ABOUT THE AUTHOR

Bruce Betts, Ph.D., is a planetary scientist and children's book author who loves teaching people about planets, space, and the night sky in fun and entertaining ways. He is the author of *Astronomy for Kids*, *Super Cool Space Facts*, *My First Book of Planets*, and *V.R. Space Explorers: Titan's Black Cat*.

Bruce has lots of college degrees, lots of big dogs, and two sons. He is the chief scientist and LightSail Program manager for the world's largest space interest group, The Planetary Society. He has a BS and an MS from Stanford and a planetary science PhD from the California Institute of Technology (a.k.a. Caltech). His research there and at the Planetary Science Institute focused on infrared studies of planetary surfaces. He managed planetary instrument development programs at NASA Headquarters.

Follow him on Twitter @RandomSpaceFact, Facebook under DrBruceBetts, or check his website RandomSpaceFact.com.